The Double Dream of Spring

Also by John Ashbery

The
Double Dream
of Spring

JOHN ASHBERY

THE ECCO PRESS
NEW YORK

LIBRARY OF CONGRESS CATALOGING IN PUBLICATION DATA
Ashbery, John.
    The double dream of spring.
    I. Title.
PS3501.S475D6   1976   811'.5'4   75-34557
ISBN 0-912-94627-x -ppbd.
    912-94630-x -hdbd.

Printed in U.S.A.

Acknowledgment is hereby made to the following publications in which these poems first appeared: *Angel Hair:* "The Hod Carrier"; *Art and Literature:* "French Poems"; *Best in Company:* "Variations, Calypso and Fugue on a Theme of Ella Wheeler Wilcox"; *Cicada:* "Song"; *The Columbia Forum:* "Parergon"; *Extensions:* "Years of Indiscretion," "Young Man with Letter"; *Harper's Magazine:* "Clouds," "Summer"; *New American Review:* "Decoy," "Evening in the Country"; *Paris Review:* "The Bungalows," "The Chateau Hardware," "Farm Implements and Rutabagas in a Landscape," "Plainness in Diversity," "Soonest Mended," "Spring Day," "The Task"; *Poetry:* "An Outing," "For John Clare," "Fragment," "It Was Raining in the Capital," "Sortes Vergilianae"; *Sunrise in Suburbia:* "Sunrise in Suburbia" published by Phoenix Bookshop; *Times Literary Supplement:* "Definition of Blue"; *TriQuarterly:* "The Double Dream of Spring," "Rural Objects."

Second printing

Acknowledgments

I am grateful to Mrs. Fritz Benedict of Aspen, Colorado, daughter of Arthur Cravan, for permission to publish a translation of the latter's poem, "Des Paroles."

I also wish to thank the Guggenheim Foundation for a grant which was of great help in writing this book.

J. A.

Contents

The Double Dream of Spring

The Task

They are preparing to begin again:
Problems, new pennant up the flagpole
In a predicated romance.

About the time the sun begins to cut laterally across
The western hemisphere with its shadows, its carnival echoes,
The fugitive lands crowd under separate names.
It is the blankness that succeeds gaiety, and Everyman must depart
Out there into stranded night, for his destiny
Is to return unfruitful out of the lightness
That passing time evokes. It was only
Cloud-castles, adept to seize the past
And possess it, through hurting. And the way is clear
Now for linear acting into that time
In whose corrosive mass he first discovered how to breathe.

Just look at the filth you've made,
See what you've done.
Yet if these are regrets they stir only lightly
The children playing after supper,
Promise of the pillow and so much in the night to come.
I plan to stay here a little while
For these are moments only, moments of insight,
And there are reaches to be attained,
A last level of anxiety that melts
In becoming, like miles under the pilgrim's feet.

Spring Day

The immense hope, and forbearance
Trailing out of night, to sidewalks of the day
Like air breathed into a paper city, exhaled
As night returns bringing doubts

That swarm around the sleeper's head
But are fended off with clubs and knives, so that morning
Installs again in cold hope
The air that was yesterday, is what you are,

In so many phases the head slips from the hand.
The tears ride freely, laughs or sobs:
What do they matter? There is free giving and taking;
The giant body relaxed as though beside a stream

Wakens to the force of it and has to recognize
The secret sweetness before it turns into life—
Sucked out of many exchanges, torn from the womb,
Disinterred before completely dead—and heaves

Its mountain-broad chest. "They were long in coming,
Those others, and mattered so little that it slowed them
To almost nothing. They were presumed dead,
Their names honorably grafted on the landscape

To be a memory to men. Until today
We have been living in their shell.
Now we break forth like a river breaking through a dam,
Pausing over the puzzled, frightened plain,

And our further progress shall be terrible,
Turning fresh knives in the wounds
In that gulf of recreation, that bare canvas
As matter-of-fact as the traffic and the day's noise."

The mountain stopped shaking; its body
Arched into its own contradiction, its enjoyment,
As far from us lights were put out, memories of boys and girls
Who walked here before the great change,

Before the air mirrored us,
Taking the opposite shape of our effort,
Its inseparable comment and corollary
But casting us further and further out.

Wha—what happened? You are with
The orange tree, so that its summer produce
Can go back to where we got it wrong, then drip gently
Into history, if it wants to. A page turned; we were

Just now floundering in the wind of its colossal death.
And whether it is Thursday, or the day is stormy,
With thunder and rain, or the birds attack each other,
We have rolled into another dream.

No use charging the barriers of that other:
It no longer exists. But you,
Gracious and growing thing, with those leaves like stars,
We shall soon give all our attention to you.

Plainness in Diversity

Silly girls your heads full of boys
There is a last sample of talk on the outer side
Your stand at last lifts to dumb evening
It is reflected in the steep blue sides of the crater,
So much water shall wash over these our breaths
Yet shall remain unwashed at the end. The fine
Branches of the fir tree catch at it, ebbing.
Not on our planet is the destiny
That can make you one.

To be placed on the side of some mountain
Is the truer story, with the breath only
Coming in patches at first, and then the little spurt
The way a steam engine starts up eventually.
The sagas purposely ignore how better off it was next day,
The feeling in between the chapters, like fins.
There is so much they must say, and it is important
About all the swimming motions, and the way the hands
Came up out of the ocean with original fronds,
The famous arrow, the girls who came at dawn
To pay a visit to the young child, and how, when he grew up to be
    a man
The same restive ceremony replaced the limited years between,
Only now he was old, and forced to begin the journey to the sun.

Soonest Mended

Barely tolerated, living on the margin
In our technological society, we were always having to be rescued
On the brink of destruction, like heroines in *Orlando Furioso*
Before it was time to start all over again.
There would be thunder in the bushes, a rustling of coils,
And Angelica, in the Ingres painting, was considering
The colorful but small monster near her toe, as though wondering
    whether forgetting
The whole thing might not, in the end, be the only solution.
And then there always came a time when
Happy Hooligan in his rusted green automobile
Came plowing down the course, just to make sure everything was
    O.K.,
Only by that time we were in another chapter and confused
About how to receive this latest piece of information.
Was it information? Weren't we rather acting this out
For someone else's benefit, thoughts in a mind
With room enough and to spare for our little problems (so they began
    to seem),
Our daily quandary about food and the rent and bills to be paid?
To reduce all this to a small variant,
To step free at last, minuscule on the gigantic plateau—
This was our ambition: to be small and clear and free.
Alas, the summer's energy wanes quickly,
A moment and it is gone. And no longer
May we make the necessary arrangements, simple as they are.
Our star was brighter perhaps when it had water in it.
Now there is no question even of that, but only
Of holding on to the hard earth so as not to get thrown off,

With an occasional dream, a vision: a robin flies across
The upper corner of the window, you brush your hair away
And cannot quite see, or a wound will flash
Against the sweet faces of the others, something like:
This is what you wanted to hear, so why
Did you think of listening to something else? We are all talkers
It is true, but underneath the talk lies
The moving and not wanting to be moved, the loose
Meaning, untidy and simple like a threshing floor.

These then were some hazards of the course,
Yet though we knew the course *was* hazards and nothing else
It was still a shock when, almost a quarter of a century later,
The clarity of the rules dawned on you for the first time.
They were the players, and we who had struggled at the game
Were merely spectators, though subject to its vicissitudes
And moving with it out of the tearful stadium, borne on shoulders,
    at last.
Night after night this message returns, repeated
In the flickering bulbs of the sky, raised past us, taken away from us,
Yet ours over and over until the end that is past truth,
The being of our sentences, in the climate that fostered them,
Not ours to own, like a book, but to be with, and sometimes
To be without, alone and desperate.
But the fantasy makes it ours, a kind of fence-sitting
Raised to the level of an esthetic ideal. These were moments, years,
Solid with reality, faces, namable events, kisses, heroic acts,
But like the friendly beginning of a geometrical progression
Not too reassuring, as though meaning could be cast aside some day
When it had been outgrown. Better, you said, to stay cowering
Like this in the early lessons, since the promise of learning
Is a delusion, and I agreed, adding that
Tomorrow would alter the sense of what had already been learned,

That the learning process is extended in this way, so that from this
    standpoint
None of us ever graduates from college,
For time is an emulsion, and probably thinking not to grow up
Is the brightest kind of maturity for us, right now at any rate.
And you see, both of us were right, though nothing
Has somehow come to nothing; the avatars
Of our conforming to the rules and living
Around the home have made—well, in a sense, "good citizens" of us,
Brushing the teeth and all that, and learning to accept
The charity of the hard moments as they are doled out,
For this is action, this not being sure, this careless
Preparing, sowing the seeds crooked in the furrow,
Making ready to forget, and always coming back
To the mooring of starting out, that day so long ago.

Summer

There is that sound like the wind
Forgetting in the branches that means something
Nobody can translate. And there is the sobering "later on,"
When you consider what a thing meant, and put it down.

For the time being the shadow is ample
And hardly seen, divided among the twigs of a tree,
The trees of a forest, just as life is divided up
Between you and me, and among all the others out there.

And the thinning-out phase follows
The period of reflection. And suddenly, to be dying
Is not a little or mean or cheap thing,
Only wearying, the heat unbearable,

And also the little mindless constructions put upon
Our fantasies of what we did: summer, the ball of pine needles,
The loose fates serving our acts, with token smiles,
Carrying out their instructions too accurately—

Too late to cancel them now—and winter, the twitter
Of cold stars at the pane, that describes with broad gestures
This state of being that is not so big after all.
Summer involves going down as a steep flight of steps

To a narrow ledge over the water. Is this it, then,
This iron comfort, these reasonable taboos,
Or did you mean it when you stopped? And the face
Resembles yours, the one reflected in the water.

It Was Raining in the Capital

It was raining in the capital
And for many days and nights
The one they called the Aquarian
Had stayed alone with her delight.

What with the winter and its business
It had fallen to one side
And she had only recently picked it up
Where the other had died.

Between the pages of the newspaper
It smiled like a face.
Next to the drugstore on the corner
It looked to another place.

Or it would just hang around
Like sullen clouds over the sun.
But—this was the point—it was real
To her and to everyone.

For spring had entered the capital
Walking on gigantic feet.
The smell of witch hazel indoors
Changed to narcissus in the street.

She thought she had seen all this before:
Bundles of new, fresh flowers,
All changing, pressing upward
To the distant office towers.

Until now nothing had been easy,
Hemmed in by all that shit—
Horseshit, dogshit, birdshit, manshit—
Yes, she remembered having said it,

Having spoken in that way, thinking
There could be no road ahead,
Sobbing into the intractable presence of it
As one weeps alone in bed.

Its chamber was narrower than a seed
Yet when the doorbell rang
It reduced all that living to air
As *"kyrie eleison"* it sang.

Hearing that music he had once known
But now forgotten, the man,
The one who had waited casually in the dark
Turned to smile at the door's span.

He smiled and shrugged—a lesson
In the newspaper no longer
But fed by the ink and paper
Into a sign of something stronger

Who reads the news and takes the bus
Going to work each day
But who was never born of woman
Nor formed of the earth's clay.

Then what unholy bridegroom
Did the Aquarian foretell?
Or was such lively intelligence
Only the breath of hell?

It scarcely mattered at the moment
And it shall never matter at all
Since the moment will not be replaced
But stand, poised for its fall,

Forever. "This is what my learning
Teaches," the Aquarian said,
"To absorb life through the pores
For the life around you is dead."

The sun came out in the capital
Just before it set.
The lovely death's head shone in the sky
As though these two had never met.

Variations, Calypso and Fugue
on a Theme of Ella Wheeler Wilcox

"For the pleasures of the many
May be ofttimes traced to one
As the hand that plants an acorn
Shelters armies from the sun."
And in places where the annual rainfall is .0071 inches
What a pleasure to lie under the tree, to sit, stand, and get up under
    the tree!
Im wunderschönen Monat Mai
The feeling is of never wanting to leave the tree,
Of predominantly peace and relaxation.
Do you step out from under the shade a moment,
It is only to return with renewed expectation, of expectation fulfilled.
Insecurity be damned! There is something to all this, that will not
    elude us:
Growing up under the shade of friendly trees, with our brothers all
    around.
And truly, young adulthood was never like this:
Such delight, such consideration, such affirmation in the way the day
    goes 'round together.
Yes, the world goes 'round a good deal faster
When there are highlights on the lips, unspoken and true words in
    the heart,
And the hand keeps brushing away a strand of chestnut hair, only
    to have it fall back into place again.
But all good things must come to an end, and so one must move
    forward
Into the space left by one's conclusions. Is this growing old?

Well, it is a good experience, to divest oneself of some tested ideals,
   some old standbys,
And even finding nothing to put in their place is a good experience,
Preparing one, as it does, for the consternation that is to come.
But—and this is the gist of it—what if I dreamed it all,
The branches, the late afternoon sun,
The trusting camaraderie, the love that watered all,
Disappearing promptly down into the roots as it should?
For later in the vast gloom of cities, only there you learn
How the ideas were good only because they had to die,
Leaving you alone and skinless, a drawing by Vesalius.
This is what was meant, and toward which everything directs:
That the tree should shrivel in 120-degree heat, the acorns
Lie around on the worn earth like eyeballs, and the lead soldiers
   shrug and slink off.

So my youth was spent, underneath the trees
I always moved around with perfect ease

I voyaged to Paris at the age of ten
And met many prominent literary men

Gazing at the Alps was quite a sight
I felt the tears flow forth with all their might

A climb to the Acropolis meant a lot to me
I had read the Greek philosophers you see

In the Colosseum I thought my heart would burst
Thinking of all the victims who had been there first

On Mount Ararat's side I began to grow
Remembering the Flood there, so long ago

On the banks of the Ganges I stood in mud
And watched the water light up like blood

The Great Wall of China is really a thrill
It cleaves through the air like a silver pill

It was built by the hand of man for good or ill
Showing what he can do when he decides not to kill

But of all the sights that were seen by me
In the East or West, on land or sea,
The best was the place that is spelled H-O-M-E.

Now that once again I have achieved home
I shall forbear all further urge to roam

There is a hole of truth in the green earth's rug
Once you find it you are as snug as a bug

Maybe some do not like it quite as much as you
That isn't all you're going to do.

You must remember that it is yours
Which is why nobody is sending you flowers

This age-old truth I to thee impart
Act according to the dictates of your art

Because if you don't no one else is going to
And that person isn't likely to be you.

It is the wind that comes from afar
It is the truth of the farthest star

In all likelihood you will not need these
So take it easy and learn your ABC's

And trust in the dream that will never come true
'Cause that is the scheme that is best for you
And the gleam that is the most suitable too.

"MAKE MY DREAM COME TRUE." This message, set in 84-point
Hobo type, startled in the morning editions of the paper: the old,
half-won security troubles the new pause. And with the approach of
the holidays, the present is clearly here to stay: the big brass band of
its particular moment's consciousness invades the plazas and the
narrow alleys. Three-fourths of the houses in this city are on narrow
stilts, finer than a girl's wrists: it is largely a question of keeping one's
feet dry, and of privacy. In the morning you forget what the punish-
ment was. Probably it was something like eating a pretzel or going
into the back yard. Still, you can't tell. These things could be a lot
clearer without hurting anybody. But it does not follow that such
issues will produce the most dynamic capital gains for you.

Friday. We are really missing you.

"The most suitable," however, was not the one specially asked for
nor the one hanging around the lobby. It was just the one asked after,
day after day—what spilled over, claimed by the spillway. The dis-
tinction of a dog, of how a dog walks. The thought of a dog walking.
No one ever referred to the incident again. The case was officially
closed. Maybe there were choruses of silent gratitude, welling up in
the spring night like a column of cloud, reaching to the very rafters
of the sky—but this was their own business. The point is no ear ever
heard them. Thus, the incident, to call it by one of its names—choice,
conduct, absent-minded frown might be others—came to be not only
as though it had never happened, but as though it never *could* have

happened. Sealed into the wall of all that season's coming on. And thus, for a mere handful of people—roustabouts and degenerates, most of them—it became the only true version. Nothing else mattered. It was bread by morning and night, the dates falling listlessly from the trees—man, woman, child, festering glistering in a single orb. The reply to "hello."

> Pink purple and blue
> The way you used to do

The next two days passed oddly for Peter and Christine, and were among the most absorbing they had ever known. On the one hand, a vast open basin—or sea; on the other a narrow spit of land, terminating in a copse, with a few broken-down outbuildings lying here and there. It made no difference that the bey—b-e-y this time, oriental potentate—had ordained their release, there was this funny feeling that.they should always be there, sustained by looks out over the ether, missing Mother and Alan and the others but really quiet, in a kind of activity that offers its own way of life, sunflower chained to the sun. Can it ever be resolved? Or are the forms of a person's thoughts controlled by inexorable laws, as in Dürer's Adam and Eve? So mutually exclusive, and so steep—Himalayas jammed side by side like New York apartment buildings. Oh the blame of it, the de-crescendo. My vice is worry. Forget it. The continual splitting up, the ear-shattering volumes of a polar ice-cap breaking up are just what you wanted. You've got it, so shut up.

> The crystal haze
> For days and days

Lots of sleep is an important factor, and rubbing the eyes. Getting off the subway he suddenly felt hungry. He went into one place, a place he knew, and ordered a hamburger and a cup of coffee. He hadn't been in this neighborhood in a long time—not since he was a kid. He used to play stickball in the vacant lot across the street. Sometimes his bunch would get into a fight with some of the older boys, and he'd go home tired and bleeding. Most days were the same though. He'd say "Hi" to the other kids and they'd say "Hi" to him. Nice bunch of guys. Finally he decided to take a turn past the old grade school he'd attended as a kid. It was a rambling structure of yellow brick, now gone in seediness and shabbiness which the late-afternoon shadows mercifully softened. The gravel playground in front was choked with weeds. Large trees and shrubbery would do no harm flanking the main entrance. Time farted.

> The first shock rattles the cruets in their stand,
> The second rips the door from its hinges.

"My dear friend," he said gently, "you said you were Professor Hertz. You must pardon me if I say that the information startles and mystifies me. When you are stronger I have some questions to ask you, if you will be kind enough to answer them."

No one was prepared for the man's answer to that apparently harmless statement.

Weak as he was, Gustavus Hertz raised himself on his elbow. He stared wildly about him, peering fearfully into the shadowy corners of the room.

"I will tell you nothing! Nothing, do you hear?" he shrieked. "Go away! Go away!"

Song

The song tells us of our old way of living,
Of life in former times. Fragrance of florals,
How things merely ended when they ended,
Of beginning again into a sigh. Later

Some movement is reversed and the urgent masks
Speed toward a totally unexpected end
Like clocks out of control. Is this the gesture
That was meant, long ago, the curving in

Of frustrated denials, like jungle foliage
And the simplicity of the ending all to be let go
In quick, suffocating sweetness? The day
Puts toward a nothingness of sky

Its face of rusticated brick. Sooner or later,
The cars lament, the whole business will be hurled down.
Meanwhile we sit, scarcely daring to speak,
To breathe, as though this closeness cost us life.

The pretensions of a past will some day
Make it over into progress, a growing up,
As beautiful as a new history book
With uncut pages, unseen illustrations,

And the purpose of the many stops and starts will be made clear:
Backing into the old affair of not wanting to grow
Into the night, which becomes a house, a parting of the ways
Taking us far into sleep. A dumb love.

Decoy

We hold these truths to be self-evident:
That ostracism, both political and moral, has
Its place in the twentieth-century scheme of things;
That urban chaos is the problem we have been seeing into and seeing
   into,
For the factory, deadpanned by its very existence into a
Descending code of values, has moved right across the road from
   total financial upheaval
And caught regression head-on. The descending scale does not imply
A corresponding deterioration of moral values, punctuated
By acts of corporate vandalism every five years,
Like a bunch of violets pinned to a dress, that knows and ignores its
   own standing.
There is every reason to rejoice with those self-styled prophets of
   commercial disaster, those harbingers of gloom,
Over the imminent lateness of the denouement that, advancing slowly,
   never arrives,
At the same time keeping the door open to a tongue-and-cheek atti-
   tude on the part of the perpetrators,
The men who sit down to their vast desks on Monday to begin plan-
   ning the week's notations, jotting memoranda that take
Invisible form in the air, like flocks of sparrows
Above the city pavements, turning and wheeling aimlessly
But on the average directed by discernible motives.

To sum up: We are fond of plotting itineraries
And our pyramiding memories, alert as dandelion fuzz, dart from one
   pretext to the next
Seeking in occasions new sources of memories, for memory is profit

Until the day it spreads out all its accumulation, delta-like, on the
plain
For that day no good can come of remembering, and the anomalies
cancel each other out.
But until then foreshortened memories will keep us going, alive, one
to the other.

There was never any excuse for this and perhaps there need be none,
For kicking out into the morning, on the wide bed,
Waking far apart on the bed, the two of them:
Husband and wife
Man and wife

Evening in the Country

I am still completely happy.
My resolve to win further I have
Thrown out, and am charged by the thrill
Of the sun coming up. Birds and trees, houses,
These are but the stations for the new sign of being
In me that is to close late, long
After the sun has set and darkness come
To the surrounding fields and hills.
But if breath could kill, then there would not be
Such an easy time of it, with men locked back there
In the smokestacks and corruption of the city.
Now as my questioning but admiring gaze expands
To magnificent outposts, I am not so much at home
With these memorabilia of vision as on a tour
Of my remotest properties, and the eidolon
Sinks into the effective "being" of each thing,
Stump or shrub, and they carry me inside
On motionless explorations of how dense a thing can be,
How light, and these are finished before they have begun
Leaving me refreshed and somehow younger.
Night has deployed rather awesome forces
Against this state of affairs: ten thousand helmeted footsoldiers,
A Spanish armada stretching to the horizon, all
Absolutely motionless until the hour to strike
But I think there is not too much to be said or be done
And that these things eventually take care of themselves
With rest and fresh air and the outdoors, and a good view of things.
So we might pass over this to the real
Subject of our concern, and that is

Have you begun to be in the context you feel
Now that the danger has been removed?
Light falls on your shoulders, as is its way,
And the process of purification continues happily,
Unimpeded, but has the motion started
That is to quiver your head, send anxious beams
Into the dusty corners of the rooms
Eventually shoot out over the landscape
In stars and bursts? For other than this we know nothing
And space is a coffin, and the sky will put out the light.
I see you eager in your wishing it the way
We may join it, if it passes close enough:
This sets the seal of distinction on the success or failure of your
    attempt.
There is growing in that knowledge
We may perhaps remain here, cautious yet free
On the edge, as it rolls its unblinking chariot
Into the vast open, the incredible violence and yielding
Turmoil that is to be our route.

For John Clare

Kind of empty in the way it sees everything, the earth gets to its feet
and salutes the sky. More of a success at it this time than most others
it is. The feeling that the sky might be in the back of someone's mind.
Then there is no telling how many there are. They grace everything—
bush and tree—to take the roisterer's mind off his caroling—so it's
like a smooth switch back. To what was aired in their previous connip-
tion fit. There is so much to be seen everywhere that it's like not get-
ting used to it, only there is so much it never feels new, never any
different. You are standing looking at that building and you cannot
take it all in, certain details are already hazy and the mind boggles.
What will it all be like in five years' time when you try to remember?
Will there have been boards in between the grass part and the edge
of the street? As long as that couple is stopping to look in that window
over there we cannot go. We feel like they have to tell us we can, but
they never look our way and they are already gone, gone far into the
future—the night of time. If we could look at a photograph of it and
say there they are, they never really stopped but there they are. There
is so much to be said, and on the surface of it very little gets said.

There ought to be room for more things, for a spreading out, like.
Being immersed in the details of rock and field and slope—letting
them come to you for once, and then meeting them halfway would
be so much easier—if they took an ingenuous pride in being in one's
blood. Alas, we perceive them if at all as those things that were meant
to be put aside—costumes of the supporting actors or voice trilling at
the end of a narrow enclosed street. You can do nothing with them.
Not even offer to pay.

It is possible that finally, like coming to the end of a long, barely
perceptible rise, there is mutual cohesion and interaction. The whole
scene is fixed in your mind, the music all present, as though you could

see each note as well as hear it. I say this because there is an uneasiness in things just now. Waiting for something to be over before you are forced to notice it. The pollarded trees scarcely bucking the wind —and yet it's keen, it makes you fall over. Clabbered sky. Seasons that pass with a rush. After all it's their time too—nothing says they aren't to make something of it. As for Jenny Wren, she cares, hopping about on her little twig like she was tryin' to tell us somethin', but that's just it, she couldn't even if she wanted to—dumb bird. But the others—and they in some way must know too—it would never occur to them to want to, even if they could take the first step of the terrible journey toward feeling somebody should act, that ends in utter confusion and hopelessness, east of the sun and west of the moon. So their comment is: "No comment." Meanwhile the whole history of probabilities is coming to life, starting in the upper left-hand corner, like a sail.

French Poems

for Anne and Rodrigo Moynihan

1.

The sources of these things being very distant
It is appropriate to find them, which is why mist
And night have "affixed the seals" to all the ardor
Of the secret of the search. Not to confound it
But to assure its living aeration.

And yet it is more in the mass
Of the mist that some day the same contacts
Will be able to unfold. I am thinking of the dance of the
Solid lightning-flashes under the cold and
Haughty sky all striated with invisible marblings.

And it does seem that all the force of
The cosmic temperature lives in the form of contacts
That no intervention could resolve,
Even that of a creator returned to the desolate
Scene of this first experiment: this microcosm.

2.

All kinds of things exist, and, what is more,
Specimens of these things, which do not make themselves known.
I am speaking of the laugh of the squire and the spur
Which are like a hole in the armor of the day.
It's annoying and then it's so natural

That we experience almost no feeling
Except a certain lightness which matches
The recent closed ambiance which is, besides,
Full of attentions for us. Thus, lightness and wealth.

But the existence of all these things and especially
The amazing fullness of their number must be
For us a source of unforgettable questions:
Such as: whence does all this come? and again:
Shall I some day be a part of all this fullness?

3.

For it does seem as though everything will once again become number
        and smile
And that no hope of completing the magnitude which surrounds us
Is permitted us. But this hope (which doesn't exist) is
Precisely a form of suspended birth,
Of that *invisible light* which spatters the silence
Of our everyday festivities. A glebe which has pursued
Its intentions of duration at the same time as reinforcing
Its basic position so that it is now
A boiling crater, form of everything that is beautiful for us.

4.

Simple, the trees placed on the landscape
Like sheaves of wheat that someone might have left there.
The manure of vanished horses, the stones that imitate it,
Everything speaks of the heavens, which created this scene
For our position alone.

Now, in associating oneself too strictly with the trajectories of things
One loses that sublime hope made of the light that sprinkles the trees.
For each progress is negation, of movement and in particular of
    number.
This number having lost its indescribable fineness
Everything must be perceived as infinite quantities of things.

Everything is landscape:
Perspectives of cliffs beaten by innumerable waves,
More wheatfields than you can count, forests
With disappearing paths, stone towers
And finally and above all the great urban centers, with
Their office buildings and populations, at the center of which
We live our lives, made up of a great quantity of isolated instants
So as to be lost at the heart of a multitude of things.

5.

It is probably on one of the inside pages
That the history of his timidity will be written,
With all the libertine thoughts of a trajectory
Roughly in the shape of a heart, around a swamp
Which for many of us will be the ultimate voyage
In view of the small amount of grace which has been accorded us,

This banality which in the last analysis is our
Most precious possession, because allowing us to
Rise above ourselves, which would not be very much
Without the presence of a lot of friends and enemies, all

Willing to swear allegiance to us, entering thus
The factory of our lives. The greatest among us, counting little

On this last-minute ennoblement, remain
Colossal, our wide-brimmed hats representing
All the shame of glory, shutting us up in the idea of number:
The ether dividing our victories, past and future: teeth and blood.

The Double Dream of Spring

for Gerrit Henry

Mixed days, the mindless years, perceived
With half-parted lips
The way the breath of spring creeps up on you and floors you.
I had thought of all this years before
But now it was making no sense. And the song had finished:
This was the story.

Just as you find men with yellow hair and blue eyes
Among certain islands
The design is complete
And one keeps walking down to the shore
Footsteps searching it
Yet they can't have it can't not have the tune that way
And we keep stepping . . . down . . .
The rowboat rocked as you stepped into it. How flat its bottom
The little poles pushed away from the small waves in the water
And so outward. Yet we turn
To examine each other in the dream. Was it sap
Coursing in the tree
That made the buds stand out, each with a peculiar coherency?
For certainly the sidewalk led
To a point somewhere beyond itself
Caught, lost in millions of tree-analogies
Being the furthest step one might find.

And now amid the churring of locomotives
Moving on the land the grass lies over passive
Beetling its "end of the journey" mentality into your forehead

Like so much blond hair awash
Sick starlight on the night
That is readying its defenses again
As day comes up

Rural Objects

Wasn't there some way in which you too understood
About being there in the time as it was then?
A golden moment, full of life and health?
Why can't this moment be enough for us as we have become?

Is it because it was mostly made up of understanding
How the future would behave when we had moved on
To other lands, other suns, to say all there is time for
Because time is just what this instant is?

Even at the beginning the manner of the hourglass
Was all-severing, weaning of that delicious thread
That comes down even to us, *"Bénédiction de Dieu dans la Solitude,"*
Sand shaper, whistler of affectionate destinies, flames and fruit.

And now you are this thing that is outside me,
And how I in token of it am like you is
In place. In between are the bits of information
That circulate around you, all that ancient stuff,

Brought here, reassembled, carted off again
Into the back yard of your dream. If we are closer
To anything, it is in this sense that doesn't count,
Like the last few blank pages of a book.

This is why I look at you
With the eyes you once liked so much in animals:
When, in that sense, is it to be?
An ultimate warm day of the year

With the light unapproachable on the beaches?
In which case you return to the fork in the road
Doubtless to take the same path again? The second-time knowledge
Gives it fluency, makes it less of a choice

As you are older and in a dream touch bottom.
The laburnum darkened, denser at the deserted lake;
Mountain ash mindlessly dropping berries: to whom is all this?
I tell you, we are being called back

For having forgotten these names
For forgetting our proper names, for falling like nameless things
On unfamiliar slopes. To be seen again, churlishly into life,
Returning, as to the scene of a crime.

That is how the singer spoke,
In vague terms, but with an eternity of thirst
To end with a small tumbler of water
Or a single pink, leaning against the window frame in the bubble
    evening,

The mind of our birth. It was all sad and real.
They slept together at the commercial school.
The binding of a book made a tall V, like undone hair,
"To say all there was never time for."

It is no triumph to point out
That no accounting was ever asked.
The land lies flat under the umbrella
Of anxiety perpetually smoothed over

As though some token were required of how each
Arrived early for the appointment in different cities.

The least suspicion would have crumbled,
Positive, but in the end you were right to

Pillage and obstruct. And she
Stared at her toes. The argument
Can be brought back intact to the point
Of summarizing how it's just a cheap way

Of letting you off, and finally
How blue objects protruded out of the
Potential, dying and recoiling, returning as you meet them
Touching forever, water lifted out of the sea.

Years of Indiscretion

Whatever your eye alights on this morning is yours:
Dotted rhythms of colors as they fade to the color,
A gray agate, translucent and firm, with nothing
Beyond its purifying reach. It's all there.
These are things offered to your participation.

These pebbles in a row are the seasons.
This is a house in which you may wish to live.
There are more than any of us to choose from
But each must live its own time.

And with the urging of the year each hastens onward separately
In strange sensations of emptiness, anguish, romantic
Outbursts, visions and wraiths. One meeting
Cancels another. "The seven-league boot
Gliding hither and thither of its own accord"
Salutes these forms for what they now are:

Fables that time invents
To explain its passing. They entertain
The very young and the very old, and not
One's standing up in them to shoulder
Task and vision, vision in the form of a task
So that the present seems like yesterday
And yesterday the place where we left off a little while ago.

Farm Implements and Rutabagas in a Landscape

The first of the undecoded messages read: "Popeye sits in thunder,
Unthought of. From that shoebox of an apartment,
From livid curtain's hue, a tangram emerges: a country."
Meanwhile the Sea Hag was relaxing on a green couch: "How pleasant
To spend one's vacation *en la casa de Popeye*," she scratched
Her cleft chin's solitary hair. She remembered spinach

And was going to ask Wimpy if he had bought any spinach.
"M'love," he intercepted, "the plains are decked out in thunder
Today, and it shall be as you wish." He scratched
The part of his head under his hat. The apartment
Seemed to grow smaller. "But what if no pleasant
Inspiration plunge us now to the stars? *For this is my country.*"

Suddenly they remembered how it was cheaper in the country.
Wimpy was thoughtfully cutting open a number 2 can of spinach
When the door opened and Swee'pea crept in. "How pleasant!"
But Swee'pea looked morose. A note was pinned to his bib. "Thunder
And tears are unavailing," it read. "Henceforth shall Popeye's
    apartment
Be but remembered space, toxic or salubrious, whole or scratched."

Olive came hurtling through the window; its geraniums scratched
Her long thigh. "I have news!" she gasped. "Popeye, forced as you
    know to flee the country
One musty gusty evening, by the schemes of his wizened, duplicate
    father, jealous of the apartment
And all that it contains, myself and spinach

In particular, heaves bolts of loving thunder
At his own astonished becoming, rupturing the pleasant

Arpeggio of our years. No more shall pleasant
Rays of the sun refresh your sense of growing old, nor the scratched
Tree-trunks and mossy foliage, only immaculate darkness and
  thunder."
She grabbed Swee'pea. "I'm taking the brat to the country."
"But you can't do that—he hasn't even finished his spinach,"
Urged the Sea Hag, looking fearfully around at the apartment.

But Olive was already out of earshot. Now the apartment
Succumbed to a strange new hush. "Actually it's quite pleasant
Here," thought the Sea Hag. "If this is all we need fear from spinach
Then I don't mind so much. Perhaps we could invite Alice the Goon
  over"—she scratched
One dug pensively—"but Wimpy is such a country
Bumpkin, always burping like that." Minute at first, the thunder

Soon filled the apartment. It was domestic thunder,
The color of spinach. Popeye chuckled and scratched
His balls: it sure was pleasant to spend a day in the country.

Sunrise in Suburbia

The tone is hard is heard
Is the coming of strength out of night: unfeared;
Still the colors are there and they
Ask the question of this what is to be
Out of a desert of chance in which being is life
But like a paradox, death reinforcing the life,
Sound under memory, as though our right to hear
Hid old unwillingness to continue
Or a style of turning to the window
Hands directing the air, and no design sticks,
Only agreement not to let it die.

Others will bend these as it is possible
And a new mode will be sunning into the past:
Refreshment and ease to the statement
And back to the safe beginning, because it starts out
Once more, drawn to and fro in a warm current of breathing
As fires start in hope and cold and
Color those nearest and only warm the most distant.
The inflection is suspended,
Not to be thoroughly initiated, under a spell to continue;
Its articulate flatness, goal, barrier and climate.

Through the clutter of
The unbound year, the first dazed marks of waking
Stir on the cloud-face like texture of paper, breath at elbow
And the collapsed sign of yesterday afternoon, its
Variance put up like a shutter,
Taxing you into January of stomping, cursing and the breath-bite.

The entrance you need is
Sideways in pentagonal fields cursive in advance
Before the fathoming of spring and
Sound let deep into the flank of occurrence
As maps lean south and shrivel toward the north.

It is fine to be in on it, stone markings, always
And eventually at some limit with a high view
But cross-country skirtings were part of the next lesson
That sleep evades, and in him was no parking space
For looks dragged under windows next time, from boarded-up places
Speaking no mind into the center of the rout.

And as day followed day the plainer meaning of it
Became a constant projected on the emigration.
The tundra seemed elaborated.
Then a permanent falling back shapes, signs the residue
As a tiny wood fence's the signature of disgust and decay
On an otherwise concerned but unmoved, specially obtruded hill:
Flatness of what remains
And modelling of what fled,
Decisions for a proper ramble into known but unimaginable, dense
Fringe expecting night,
A light wilderness of spoken words not
Unkind for all their aimlessness,
A blank chart of each day moving into the premise of difficult visibility
And which is nowhere, the urge to nowhere,
To retract that statement, sharply, within the next few minutes.
For it is as though it turns you back,
Your eyes through the recent happenings as they advance through you,
Never satisfied on the way, but
There is reasonable assurance in the way it is not seen again,
Banging of the shuttle, repeated swipes of the wind,

For the afterthought coincides: much of it was intentional.
It is aloes to be remembered toward the place
Out of which it grew like forest out of mountain, when later someone
    says there was no mountain
Only roads, and stars hanging over them,
Only a flat stone over the place where it says there is more.

It is a low game, too tired to sleep,
Feeling through equipment to the less developed:
"You've gone and mixed me up
I was happy just bumming along,
Any old way, in and out, up and down."
The passion has left his head, and the head reports.

And then some morning there is a nuance:
Suddenly in the city dirt and varied
Ideas of rubbish, the blue day stands and
A sudden interest is there:
Lying on the cot, near the tree-shadow,
Out of the thirties having news of the true source:
Face to kiss and the wonderful hair curling down
Into margins that care and are swept up again like branches
Into actual closeness
And the little things that lighten the day
The kindness of acts long forgotten
Which give us history and faith
And parting at night, next to oceans, like the collapse of dying.
It is all noticed before it is too late
But its immobility gives no comfort, only chapter headings and folio
    numbers
And it can go on being divine in itself
Neither treasured nor cast down in anger
For we cannot imagine the truth of it.

This deaf rasping of branch against branch
Like a noncommittal sneer among many superimposed chimes
As we go separate ways
That have translated the foreground of paths into quoted spaces:
They are empty beyond consternation because
These are the droppings of all our lives
And they recall no past de luxe quarters
Only a last cube.
The thieves were not breaking in, the castle was not being stormed.
It was the holiness of the day that fed our notions
And released them, sly breath of Eros,
Anniversary on the woven city lament, that assures our arriving
In hours, seconds, breath, watching our salary
In the morning holocaust become one vast furnace, engaging all tears.

Definition of Blue

The rise of capitalism parallels the advance of romanticism
And the individual is dominant until the close of the nineteenth
  century.
In our own time, mass practices have sought to submerge the per-
  sonality
By ignoring it, which has caused it instead to branch out in all directions
Far from the permanent tug that used to be its notion of "home."
These different impetuses are received from everywhere
And are as instantly snapped back, hitting through the cold atmosphere
In one steady, intense line.

There is no remedy for this "packaging" which has supplanted the old
  sensations.
Formerly there would have been architectural screens at the point
  where the action became most difficult
As a path trails off into shrubbery—confusing, forgotten, yet continu-
  ing to exist.
But today there is no point in looking to imaginative new methods
Since all of them are in constant use. The most that can be said for
  them further
Is that erosion produces a kind of dust or exaggerated pumice
Which fills space and transforms it, becoming a medium
In which it is possible to recognize oneself.

Each new diversion adds its accurate touch to the ensemble, and so
A portrait, smooth as glass, is built up out of multiple corrections
And it has no relation to the space or time in which it was lived.
Only its existence is a part of all being, and is therefore, I suppose, to
  be prized

Beyond chasms of night that fight us
By being hidden and present.

And yet it results in a downward motion, or rather a floating one
In which the blue surroundings drift slowly up and past you
To realize themselves some day, while, you, in this nether world that
could not be better
Waken each morning to the exact value of what you did and said,
which remains.

Parergon

We are happy in our way of life.
It doesn't make much sense to others. We sit about,
Read, and are restless. Occasionally it becomes time
To lower the dark shade over it all.
Our entity pivots on a self-induced trance
Like sleep. Noiseless our living stops
And one strays as in a dream
Into those respectable purlieus where life is motionless and alive
To utter the few words one knows:

"O woebegone people! Why so much crying,
Such desolation in the streets?
Is it the present of flesh, that each of you
At your jagged casement window should handle,
Nervous unto thirst and ultimate death?
Meanwhile the true way is sleeping;
Your lawful acts drink an unhealthy repose
From the upturned lip of this vessel, secretly,
But it is always time for a change.
That certain sins of omission go unpunished
Does not weaken your position
But this underbrush in which you are secure
Is its doing. Farewell then,
Until, under a better sky
We may meet expended, for just doing it
Is only an excuse. We need the tether
Of entering each other's lives, eyes wide apart, crying."

As one who moves forward from a dream
The stranger left that house on hastening feet

Leaving behind the woman with the face shaped like an arrowhead,
And all who gazed upon him wondered at
The strange activity around him.
How fast the faces kindled as he passed!
It was a marvel that no one spoke
To stem the river of his passing
Now grown to flood proportions, as on the sunlit mall
Or in the enclosure of some court
He took his pleasure, savage
And mild with the contemplating.
Yet each knew he saw only aspects,
That the continuity was fierce beyond all dream of enduring,
And turned his head away, and so
The lesson eddied far into the night:
Joyful its beams, and in the blackness blacker still,
Though undying joyousness, caught in that trap.

The Hod Carrier

You have been declining the land's
Breakable extensions, median whose face is half my face.
Your curved visor's the supposition that unites us.

                              I've been thinking about you

After a dry summer, fucking in the autumn,
Reflecting among arabesques of speech that arise
The certain anomaly, the wise smile
Of winter fitted over the land
And your activity disappears in mist, or translates too easily
Into a general puree, someone's aura or idea of games—
The stone you cannot perfect, the sharp iron blade you cannot prevent.

But this new way we are, the melon head
Half-mirrored, the way sentences suddenly spurt up like gas
Or sting and jab, is it that we accepted each complication
As it came along, and are therefore happy with the result?
Or was it as a condition of seeing
That we vouchsafed aid and comfort to the seasons

                              As each came begging

And the present, so flat in its belief, so "outside it"
As it maintains, becomes the blind side of
The fulfillment of that condition; and work, ripeness
And tired but resolute standing up for one's rights
Mean leaning toward the stars

                    The way a tree leans toward the sun

Not meaning to get close

                  And the bird walked right up that tree.

You have reached the point closest to your destination

                  O tired beacon
                  Dominating the plain
                  Yet all but invisible

To the mind surrounding your purpose
You are totally subsumed
The good abstracted, squandered, thrown away
As it was in the lean time.
Are these floorboards, to be stared at
In moments of guilt, as wallpaper can stream away and yet

                  You cannot declare it?

Then each breath is a redeeming feature
Resolving in alteration
The inanity of flowers into perfect conditions
That their mildness can only postpone, not change.

And surveying the hundredfold record of the summer
The shapely witness declares herself at last
Content with the result:
Whitecaps wincing at every point of the compass
The justified demands of commerce, difficult departures and all
Into a hemisphere where no credit is expected
And the shipping is rendered into its own terms.

                  It is what keeps itself
                  From going blind

All aging is perpetual chatter
On these buff planes, protuberances
And you are in the wind at night

        And so it is an even darker night

And death is the prevention of which the cure's
Metal polish and sawdust

        Light grinding into your heels.

An Outing

"These things . . . that you are going to have—
Are you paid specially for them?"

                    "Yes."

"And when it is over, do you insist,
Do you insist that the visitor leave the room?"
"My activity is as random as the wind.
Why should I insist? The visitor is free to go,
Or to stay, as he chooses."

Are you folks just going out for a walk
And if you are would you check the time
On your way back? It's too late to do anything today.
I would just take a pratfall if I stepped outside that door.

"I don't know whether I should apply or nothing."
"I think you shd make yr decision."

So it was by chance we found ourselves
Gumshod on the pebbled path, Denmark O Denmark
Flat, rounded eyes, Denmark Denmark
Gray parchment landscape Denmark O Denmark
Unmanageable sky, Denmark that cannot shift
The faucet drips, the minutes apply, Denmark.

Some Words

from the French of Arthur Cravan

Life is not at all what you might think it to be
A simple tale where each thing has its history
    It's much more than its scuffle and anything goes
Both evil and good, subject to the same laws.
    Each hour has its color and forever gives place
Leaving less than yon bird of itself a trace.
In vain does memory attempt to store away
The scent of its colors in a single bouquet
Memory can but shift cold ashes around
When the depths of time it endeavors to sound.
    Never think that you may be allowed, at the end,
To say to yourself, "I am of myself the friend,"
Or make with yourself a last reconciliation.
You will remain the victim of your hesitation
You will forget today before tomorrow is here
And disavow yourself while much is still far from clear.
    The defunct days will offer you their images
Only so that you may read of former outrages
And the days to come will mar with their complaints
The splendor that in your honor dejected evening paints.
    Wishing to collect in your heart the feelings
Scattered in the meadows of misfortune's hard dealings
You will be the shepherd whose dog has run away
You will know even less whence comes your dismay
Than you know the hour your boredom first saw the light.
    Weary of seeking day you will relish the night
In night's dim orchards you will find some rest
The counsels of the trees of night are best

Better than those of the tree of knowledge, which corrupts us at birth
And which you allowed to flourish in the accursèd earth.
    When your most arduous labors grow pale as death
And you begin to inhale autumn's chilly breath
Winter will come soon to batter with his mace
Your precious moments, scattering them all over the place.
    You will always be having to get up from your chairs
To move on to other heartbreaks, be caught in other snares.
    The seasons will revolve on their scented course
Solar or devastated you will perforce
Be perfumed at their tepid passing, and not know
Whether their fragrance brings you joy or woe.
    At the moment when your life becomes a total shambles
You will have to resume your hopeless rambles
You have left everything behind and you still are eligible
And all alone, as the gulf becomes unbridgeable
You will have to earn your daily bread
Although you feel you'd be better off dead.
    They'll hurt you, and you'd like to put up some resistance
Because you know that your very existence
Depends on others as unworthy of you
As you are of God, and when it's time to review
Your wrongs, you will feel no pain, they will seem like a joke
For you will have ceased to suffer under their yoke.
    Whether you pass through fields, towns or across the sea
You will always retain your melancholy
And look after it; you will have to think of your career
Not live it, as in a game where the best player
Is he who forgets himself, and cannot say
What spurs him on, and makes him win the day.
    When weary henceforth of wishing to gaze
At the sinuous path of your strung-out days
You return to the place where your stables used to tower

You will find nothing left but some fetid manure
Your steeds beneath other horsemen will have fled
To autumn's far country, all rusted and red.
      Like an ardent rose in the September sun
You will feel the flesh sag from your limbs, one by one,
Less of you than of a pruned rosebush will remain,
That spring lies in wait for, to clothe once again.
      If you wish to love you won't know whom to choose
There are none whose love you'd be sorry to lose
Not to love at all would be the better part
Lest another seize and confiscate your heart.
      When evening descends on your deserted routes
You won't be afraid and will say, "What boots
It to worry and fret? To rail at my luck?
Since time my actions like an apple will pluck."
      You would like of yourself to curtail certain features
That you dislike, making allowances for this creature,
Giving that other one a chance to show his fettle,
Confining yet another behind bars of metal:
That rebel will soon become an armèd titan.
      Then let yourself love all that you take delight in
Accept yourself whole, accept the heritage
That shaped you and is passed on from age to age
Down to your entity. Remain mysterious;
Rather than be pure, accept yourself as numerous.
The wave of heredity will not be denied:
Best, then, on a lover's silken breast to abide
And be wafted by her to Nirvana's blue shoals
Where the self is abolished and renounces its goals.
      In you all things must live and procreate
Forget about the harvest and its sheaves of wheat
You are the harvest and not the reaper
And of your domain another is the keeper.

When you see the lapsed dreams that childhood invents
Salute your adolescence and fold their tents
Virginal, tall and slim beside the jasmine tree
An adorable girl is plaiting tenderly
The bouquet of love, which will stick in your memory
As the final vision and the final story.

Henceforth you will burn with lascivious fire
Accursèd passion will strum its lyre
At the charming crossroads where day is on the wane
As the curve of a hill dissolves in a plain.

The tacit beauty of the sacred plateau
Will be spoiled for you and you will never know
Henceforth the peace a pious heart bestows
To the soul its gentle sister in whom it echoes;
Anxiety will have called everything into question
And you will be tempted to the wildest actions.

Then let all fade at the edge of our days!
No God emerges to dream our destinies.
The days depart, only boredom does not retreat
It's like a path that flies beneath one's feet
Whose horizon shifts while as we trudge
The dust and mud stick to us and do not budge.

In vain do we speak, provoke actions or think,
We are prisoners of the world's demented sink.

The soft enchantments of our years of innocence
Are harvested by accredited experience
Our fondest memories soon turn to poison
And only oblivion remains in season.

When, beside a window, one feels evening prevail
Who is there who can receive its slanting veil
And not regret day that bore it on its stream
Whether day was joy or under evil's regime
Drawing us to the one and deploring the other

Regretting the departure of all our brothers
And all that made the day, including its stains.
       Whoever you may be O man who complains
Not at your destiny, can you then doubt,
When the moment arrives for you to stretch out,
That remorse, a stinking jackal with subtle nose,
Will come at the end to devour your repose?
       . . . Something gentle and something sad eftsoons
In the flanks of our pale and realistic noons
Holds with our soul a discourse without end
The curtain rises on the afternoon wind
Day sheds its leaves and now will soon be gone
And already my adulthood seems to mourn
Beside the reddish sunsets of the hollow vase
As gently it starts to deepen and slowly to increase.

Young Man with Letter

Another feeble, wonderful creature is making the rounds again,
In this phraseology we become, as clouds like leaves
Fashion the internal structure of a season
From water into ice. Such an abstract can be
Dazed waking of the words with no memory of what happened before,
Waiting for the second click. We know them well enough now,
Forever, from living into them, tender, frivolous and puzzled
And we know that with them we will come out right.

But a new question poses itself:
Is it we who are being transformed?
The light in the hallway seems to indicate it
And the corrosive friends whose breath is so close
It whistles, are changed to tattered pretexts
As a sign, perhaps, that all's well with us.
Yet the quiet bickering on the edge of morning

That advances to a steady drone by noon
And to hollow rumblings by night: is there so much good then
Blushing beyond the sense of it, standing straight up for others to view?
Is it not more likely that such straining and puffing
As commas produce, this ferment
We take as suddenly our present
Is our waltzing somewhere else, down toward the view
But holding off? The spiked neon answers it
Up against the charged black of a full sky:
"We thought you knew, brothers not ancestors;
Your time has come, has come to stay;
The sieved dark can tell you about it."

Clouds

All this time he had only been waiting,
Not even thinking, as many had supposed.
Now sleep wound down to him its promise of dazzling peace
And he stood up to assume that imagination.

There were others in the forest as close as he
To caring about the silent outcome, but they had gotten lost
In the shadows of dreams so that the external look
Of the nearby world had become confused with the cobwebs inside.

Yet all would finish at the end, or go undreamed of.
It was a solid light in which a man and woman could kiss
Yet dark and ambiguous as a cloakroom.
No noise was to underline the notion of its being.

Thus the thing grew heavy with the mere curve of being,
As a fruit ripens through the long summer before falling
Out of the idea of existence into the fact of being received,
As many another guest. And the helloes and goodbyes are never stilled;

They stay in the foreground and look back on it.
It was still possible of course to imagine that an era had ended,
Yet this time was marked also by new ideas of progress and decay.
The old ideals had been cast aside and people were restless for the new,

In a wholly different mass, so there was no joining,
Only separate blocks of achievement and opinion
With no relation to the conducive ether
Which surrounded everything like the clear idea of a ruler.

And it was that these finally flattened out or banded together
Through forgetting, into one contemporaneous sea
With no explanations to give. And the small enclave
Of worried continuing began again, putting forth antennae into the
  night.

How do we explain the harm, feeling
We are always the effortless discoverers of our career,
With each day digging the grave of tomorrow and at the same time
Preparing its own redemption, constantly living and dying?

How can we outsmart the sense of continuity
That eludes our steps as it prepares us
For ultimate wishful thinking once the mind has ended
Since this last thought both confines and uplifts us?

He was like a lion tracking its prey
Through days and nights, forgetful
In the delirium of arrangements.
The birds fly up out of the underbrush,

The evening swoons out of contaminated dawns,
And now whatever goes farther must be
Alien and healthy, for death is here and knowable.
Out of touch with the basic unhappiness

He shoots forward like a malignant star.
The edges of the journey are ragged.
Only the face of night begins to grow distinct
As the fainter stars call to each other and are lost.

Day re-creates his image like a snapshot:
The family and the guests are there,

The talking over there, only now it will never end.
And so cities are arranged, and oceans traversed,

And farms tilled with especial care.
This year again the corn has grown ripe and tall.
It is a perfect rebuttal of the argument. And Semele
Moves away, puzzled at the brown light above the fields.

The Bungalows

Impatient as we were for all of them to join us,
The land had not yet risen into view: gulls had swept the gray steel
    towers away
So that it profited less to go searching, away over the humming earth
Than to stay in immediate relation to these other things—boxes, store
    parts, whatever you wanted to call them—
Whose installedness was the price of further revolutions, so you knew
    this combat was the last.
And still the relationship waxed, billowed like scenery on the breeze.

They are the same aren't they,
The presumed landscape and the dream of home
Because the people are all homesick today or desperately sleeping,
Trying to remember how those rectangular shapes
Became so extraneous and so near
To create a foreground of quiet knowledge
In which youth had grown old, chanting and singing wise hymns that
Will sign for old age
And so lift up the past to be persuaded, and be put down again.

The warning is nothing more than an aspirate "h";
The problem is sketched completely, like fireworks mounted on poles:
Complexion of evening, the accurate voices of the others.
During Coca-Cola lessons it becomes patent
Of noise on the left, and we had so skipped a stage that
The great wave of the past, compounded in derision,
Submerged idea and non-dreamer alike
In falsetto starlight like "purity"

Of design that had been the first danger sign
To wash the sticky, icky stuff down the drain—pfui!

How does it feel to be outside and inside at the same time,
The delicious feeling of the air contradicting and secretly abetting
The interior warmth? But land curdles the dismay in which it's written
Bearing to a final point of folly and doom
The wisdom of these generations.
Look at what you've done to the landscape—
The ice cube, the olive—
There is a perfect tri-city mesh of things
Extending all the way along the river on both sides
With the end left for thoughts on construction
That are always turning to alps and thresholds
Above the tide of others, feeding a European moss rose without glory.

We shall very soon have the pleasure of recording
A period of unanimous tergiversation in this respect
And to make that pleasure the greater, it is worth while
At the risk of tedious iteration, to put first upon record a final protest:
Rather decaying art, genius, inspiration to hold to
An impossible "calque" of reality, than
"The new school of the trivial, rising up on the field of battle,
Something of sludge and leaf-mold," and life
Goes trickling out through the holes, like water through a sieve,
All in one direction.

You who were directionless, and thought it would solve everything if
     you found one,
What do you make of this? Just because a thing is immortal
Is that any reason to worship it? Death, after all, is immortal.
But you have gone into your houses and shut the doors, meaning
There can be no further discussion.

And the river pursues its lonely course
With the sky and the trees cast up from the landscape
For green brings unhappiness—*le vert porte malheur.*
"The chartreuse mountain on the absinthe plain
Makes the strong man's tears tumble down like rain."

All this came to pass eons ago.
Your program worked out perfectly. You even avoided
The monotony of perfection by leaving in certain flaws:
A backward way of becoming, a forced handshake,
An absent-minded smile, though in fact nothing was left to chance.
Each detail was startlingly clear, as though seen through a magnifying
    glass,
Or would have been to an ideal observer, namely yourself—
For only you could watch yourself so patiently from afar
The way God watches a sinner on the path to redemption,
Sometimes disappearing into valleys, but always *on the way,*
For it all builds up into something, meaningless or meaningful
As architecture, because planned and then abandoned when
    completed,
To live afterwards, in sunlight and shadow, a certain amount of years.
Who cares about what was there before? There is no going back,
For standing still means death, and life is moving on,
Moving on towards death. But sometimes standing still is also life.

The Chateau Hardware

It was always November there. The farms
Were a kind of precinct; a certain control
Had been exercised. The little birds
Used to collect along the fence.
It was the great "as though," the how the day went,
The excursions of the police
As I pursued my bodily functions, wanting
Neither fire nor water,
Vibrating to the distant pinch
And turning out the way I am, turning out to greet you.

Sortes Vergilianae

You have been living now for a long time and there is nothing you do not know.

Perhaps something you read in the newspaper influenced you and that was very frequently.

They have left you to think along these lines and you have gone your own way because you guessed that

Under their hiding was the secret, casual as breath, betrayed for the asking.

Then the sky opened up, revealing much more than any of you were intended to know.

It is a strange thing how fast the growth is, almost as fast as the light from polar regions

Reflected off the arctic ice-cap in summer. When you know where it is heading

You have to follow it, though at a sadly reduced rate of speed,

Hence folly and idleness, raging at the confines of some miserable sunlit alley or court.

It is the nature of these people to embrace each other, they know no other kind but themselves.

Things pass quickly out of sight and the best is to be forgotten quickly

For it is wretchedness that endures, shedding its cancerous light on all it approaches:

Words spoken in the heat of passion, that might have been retracted in good time,

All good intentions, all that was arguable. These are stilled now, as the embrace in the hollow of its flux

And can never be revived except as perverse notations on an indisputable state of things,

As conduct in the past, vanished from the reckoning long before it
was time.

Lately you've found the dull fevers still inflict their round, only they
are unassimilable

Now that newness or importance has worn away. It is with us like
day and night,

The surge upward through the grade school positioning and bursting
into soft gray blooms

Like vacuum-cleaner sweepings, the opulent fuzz of our cage, or like
an excited insect

In nervous scrimmage for the head, etching its none-too-complex
ordinances into the matter of the day.

Presently all will go off satisfied, leaving the millpond bare, a site for
new picnics,

As they came, naked, to explore all the possible grounds on which
exchanges could be set up.

It is "No Fishing" in modest capital letters, and getting out from under
the major weight of the thing

As it was being indoctrinated and dropped, heavy as a branch with
apples,

And as it started to sigh, just before tumbling into your lap, chagrined
and satisfied at the same time,

Knowing its day over and your patience only beginning, toward what
marvels of speculation, auscultation, world-view,

Satisfied with the entourage. It is this blank carcass of whims and
tentative afterthoughts

Which is being delivered into your hand like a letter some forty-odd
years after the day it was posted.

Strange, isn't it, that the message makes some sense, if only a relative
one in the larger context of message-receiving

That you will be called to account for just as the purpose of it is
becoming plain,

Being one and the same with the day it set out, though you cannot imagine this.

There was a time when the words dug in, and you laughed and joked, accomplice

Of all the possibilities of their journey through the night and the stars, creature

Who looked to the abandonment of such archaic forms as these, and meanwhile

Supported them as the tools that made you. The rut became apparent only later

And by then it was too late to check such expansive aspects as what to do while waiting

For the others to show: unfortunately no pile of tattered magazines was in evidence,

Such dramas sleeping below the surface of the everyday machinery; besides

Quality is not given to everybody, and who are you to have been supposing you had it?

So the journey grew ever slower; the battlements of the city could now be discerned from afar

But meanwhile the water was giving out and malaria had decimated their ranks and undermined their morale,

You know the story, so that if turning back was unthinkable, so was victorious conquest of the great brazen gates.

Best perhaps to fold up right here, but even that was not to be granted.

Some days later in the pulsating of orchestras someone asked for a drink:

The music stopped and those who had been confidently counting the rhythms grew pale.

This is just a footnote, though a microcosmic one perhaps, to the greater curve

Of the elaboration; it asks no place in it, only insertion *hors-texte* as the invisible notion of how that day grew

From planisphere to heaven, and what part in it all the "I" had, the
   insatiable researcher of learned trivia, bookworm,
And one who marched along with, "made common cause," yet had
   neither the gumption nor the desire to trick the thing into happening,
Only long patience, as the star climbs and sinks, leaving illumination
   to the setting sun.

Fragment

The last block is closed in April. You
See the intrusions clouding over her face
As in the memory given you of older
Permissiveness which dies in the
Falling back toward recondite ends,
The sympathy of yellow flowers.
Never mentioned in the signs of the oblong day
The saw-toothed flames and point of other
Space not given, and yet not withdrawn
And never yet imagined: a moment's commandment.

These last weeks teasing into providential
Reality: that your face, the only real beginning,
Beyond the gray of overcoat, that this first
Salutation plummet also to the end of friendship
With self alone. And in doing so open out
New passages of being among the correctness
Of familiar patterns. The stance to you
Is a fiction, to me a whole. I find
New options, white feathers, in a word what
You draw in around you to the protecting bone.

This page only is the end of nothing
To the top of that other. The purity
Of how hard it is to choose between others where
The event takes place and the outside setting.
Day covers all this with leaves, with laughter and tears.
But at night other sounds are heard
Propositions hitherto omitted in the heat

Of smoke. You can look at it all
Inside out for the emblem to become the statue
Of discipline that rode in out of the past.

Not forgetting either the chance that you
Might want to revise this version of what is
The only real one, it might be that
No real relation exists between my wish for you
To return and the movements of your arms and legs.
But my inability to accept this fact
Annihilates it. Thus
My power over you is absolute.
You exist only in me and on account of me
And my features reflect this proved compactness.

That coming together of masses coincides
With that stable emptiness, detaining
Where this energy, not yet or only partially
Distributed to the imagination creates
A claim to the sides of early autumn.
Suffocating, with remorse, and winking with it
To tablelands of disadumbrated feeling
Treetops whose mysterious hegemony concerns
Merely, by opening around factors of accident
So as to install miscellaneous control.

The part in which you read about yourself
Grew out of this. Your interpretation is
Extremely bitter and can serve no profitable end
Except continual development. Best to break off
All further choice. In
This way new symptoms of interest having a
Common source could produce their own ingenious

Way of watering into the past with its religious
Messages and burials. Out of this cold collapse
A warm and near unpolished entity could begin.

Although beyond more reacting
To this cut-and-dried symposium way of seeing things
To outflank next mediocre condition
Of storms. The hollow thus produced
A kind of cave of the winds; distribution center
Of subordinate notions to which the stag
Returns to die: the suppressed lovers.
Then ghosts of the streets
Crowding, propagating the feeling into furious
Waves from the perfunctory and debilitated sunset.

Yet no one has time for its preoccupation.
Our daily imaginings are swiftly tilted down to
Death in its various forms. We cannot keep the peace
At home, and at the same time be winning wars abroad.
And the great flower of what we have been twists
On its stem of earth, for not being
What we are to become, fated to live in
Intimidated solitude and isolation. No brother
Bearing the notion of responsibility of self
To the surrounding neighborhood lost out of being.

Slowly as from the center of some diamond
You begin to take in the world as it moves
In toward you, part of its own burden of thought, rather
Idle musing, afternoons listing toward some sullen
Unexpected end. Seen from inside all is
Abruptness. As though to get out your eye
Sharpens and sharpens these particulars; no

Longer visible, they breathe in multicolored
Parentheses, the way love in short periods
Puts everything out of focus, coming and going.

Thus your only world is an inside one
Ironically fashioned out of external phenomena
Having no rhyme or reason, and yet neither
An existence independent of foreboding and sly grief.
Nothing anybody says can make a difference; inversely
You are a victim of their lack of consequence
Buffeted by invisible winds, or yet a flame yourself
Without meaning, yet drawing satisfaction
From the crevices of that wind, living
In that flame's idealized shape and duration.

Whereas through an act of bunching this black kite
Webs all around you with coal light: wall and reef
Imbibe and the impossible saturation,
New kinds of fun, is an earnest
Of the certain future. Yet the spores of the
Difference as it's imagined flower
In complicated chains for the eyebrow, and pre-delineate
Phantom satisfaction as it would happen. This time
You get over the threshold of so much unmeaning, so much
Being, prepared for its event, the active memorial.

And more swiftly continually in evening, limpid
Storm winds, commas are dropped, the convention gapes,
Prostrated before a monument disappearing into the dark.
It would not be good to examine these ages
Except for sun flecks, little, on the golden sand
And coming to reappraisal of the distance.
The welcoming stuns the heart, iron bells

Crash through the transparent metal of the sky
Each day slowing the method of thought a little
Until oozing sap of touchable mortality, time lost and won.

Like the blood orange we have a single
Vocabulary all heart and all skin and can see
Through the dust of incisions the central perimeter
Our imaginations' orbit. Other words,
Old ways are but the trappings and appurtenances
Meant to install change around us like a grotto.
There is nothing laughable
In this. To isolate the kernel of
Our imbalance and at the same time back up carefully;
Its tulip head whole, an imagined good.

The sense of that day toward its center
Is perforated or crisscrossed with rewards
As though the stumbling that stranded me here were
The means of some spontaneity. But upper pressures
Lifted the direction of the prevailing winds
Allowing an awaited entrance down below.
Yet all is different metric system
Flapping from grace to intense surprise.
As in a tub. No candle is lit. No theory
Strap it to the maturity of surroundings.

Its landscape puts toward a pointed roof
Continuing inquiry and reappraisal of always new
Facts pushing past into bright cold
As from general spindles a waterfall of data
Is absorbed above by command. Whether construed
As lead or gold it leaves a ring
On the embellished, attendant time. The farms

Knew it, that is why they stood so still.
The gold might reverse them to fields
Of flowering sand or black, ancient and intimate.

The volcanic entrance to an antechamber
Was not what either of us meant.
More outside than before, but what is worse, outside
Within the periphery, we are confronted
With one another, and our meeting escapes through the dark
Like a well.
Our habits ask us for instructions.
The news is to return by stages
Of uncertainty, too early or too late. It is the invisible
Shapes, the bed's confusion and prattling. The late quiet.
    This is how it feels.

The pictures were really pictures
Of loving and small things. There was a winter scene
And half-hidden sketches of the other three seasons.
Autumn was a giant with a gray woollen cap.
Near him was spring, a girl in green draperies
Half sitting, half standing near the trunk of an old tree.
Summer was a band of nondescript children
Bordering the picture of winter, which was indistinct
And gray like the sky of a winter afternoon.
The other pictures told in an infinity of tiny ways

Stories of the past: separate incidents
Recounted in touching detail, or vast histories
Murmured confusingly, as though the speaker
Were choked by sighs and tears, and had forgotten
The reason why he was telling the story.
It was these finally that made the strongest

Impression, they shook you like wind
Roaring through branches with no leaves left on them.
The vagueness was bigger than life and its apotheosis
Of shining incidents, colored or dark, vivid or serious.

But now the tidings are dark in the
Expected late afternoon suddenly dipping into
Reserves of anxiety and restlessness which dutifully
Puff out these late, lax sails, pennants;
The vertical black-and-white-striped weather indicator's
One sign of triumph, a small one, to stand
For universal concessions, charters and deeds to
Wilderness or the forested sea, cord after cord
Equaling possession and possessiveness
Instantaneously extending your hesitation to an

Empire, back lands whose sparsely populated look is
Supreme dominion. It will be divided into tracks
And these be lived in the way now the lowered
Angles of this room. Waxed moustache against the impiety
Of so much air of change, but always and nowhere
A cave. Gradually old letters used as bookmarks
Inform the neighbors; an approximate version
Circulates and the incident is officially closed.
And I some joy of this have, returning to the throbbing
Mirror's stiff enclave, the sides of my face steep and overrun.

So many ways grew over to this
Mild decline. The grave of authority
Matches wits with upward-spinning lemon spirals
Telling of the influences of night, so many decisions
Not to act accruing to the outward stretches.
The civilities of day also creep

To extremities, fly on a windowpane, sweeping
The changed refuse under the rug. Just one step
Takes you into so much outside, the candor
Of what had been going on makes you pause momentarily,

A bag of October, without being able to tell it
To the others, so that it loses silence.
I haven't made clear that I want it all from you
In writing, so as to study your facial expressions
Simultaneously: hesitations, reverse darts, the sky
Of your plans run through with many sutured points.
Only in this way can a true basis for understanding be
Set up. But meanwhile if I try to turn away
Looking for my own shadow in the excess
Like quarreling jays our heads fall to in agreement.

It exposed us on a moving gangway.
Leaning from an upper story
We should not separate in misunderstanding.
Where you were going was the key to
Saturday afternoon spent in shopping and washing dishes
Just right so the newly strengthened land would
Disinter the music box what keeps happening to
The photo of a baby girl disguised as an old man
With a long white beard. What comes after
The purge, she not mentioning it yet.

This meant (and the tone voice, repeating
"He's hurt real bad" worked up the wall of celerity
To inaudible foam) all divers and all speechless
Apostrophes of solar unit stay on the bottom.
At last there was a chance to explore the forest,
Shadow of yawning magnetic poles, in which the castle

Had been inserted like an afterthought—bare walls
With somewhere a center and even further, a widening
To accommodate eventual reaction, such as ropes,
Pikes, chains of memory, of sleep, and an end of board.

The apotheosis had sunk away
As wind incarnates its glass cone
Aiming where further identifications should
Not be worked for, are reached. The whole
Is a mound of changing valors for some who
Live out as under a dome, are participated in
As the ordinary grandeur of a dome's the thing that
Keeps them living so that additional grace
Is eternal procrastination, not to be considered
Unless a description of the actual scene.

Shedding perennial beauty on angles
Of questions asked and often answered in a
Given period. It all moves more slowly, yet
The change is more complete than ever before:
A pessimistic lighting up as of autumn woods
Demanding more than ever to be considered, for full
Substance. For the calculable stutter of a laugh.
Returning late you were not surprised to meet
This gray visitor, perpendicular to the weather.
Quiet ambition of the note variously sounded.

All space was to be shut out. Now there was no
Earthly reason for living; solitude proceeded
From want of money, her quincunxes standing
To protect the stillness of the air. Darkness
Intruded everywhere. This was the first day
Of the new experience. The familiar brown trees

Stirred indifferent at their roots, deeply transformed.
Like a sail its question disappeared into
An ocean of newsprint. To be precipitated
In desire, as hats are handed. Awnings raised.

Coming in the phaeton to the end of the
Day that had served on previous occasions
An orchard diminishes the already tiny
Notion of abstract good and bad qualities
Pod of darkness which goes vociferating early
Unchangeables that in time's mire have hid weapons.
Past waterfall wooden huts open places
Assaulted by the wind, the usual surroundings chafed
Foreknowledge of the immense journey, as the sea
Flattens, uncritical, beyond wide docks.

To persist in the revision of very old
Studies, as though mounted on a charger,
With the door to the next room partly open
To the borrowed density, what keeps happening to
So much dead surprise, a weight of spring.
An odor of explosives hangs over the change,
Now at its apogee. This presupposes a will
To carry out all instructions, dotting the last i
Though cancelling with one stroke of a pen all
The provisions, revisions and so on made until now.

But why should the present seem so particularly urgent?
A time of spotted lakes and the whippoorwill
Sounding over everything? To release the importance
Of what will always remain invisible?
In spite of near and distant events, gladly
Built? To speak the plaits of argument,

Loosened? Vast shadows are pushed down toward
The hour. It is ideation, incrimination
Proceeding from necessity to find it at
A time of day, beside the creek, uncounted stars and buttons.

We talked, and after that went out.
It was nice. There was lots of time left
And we could always come back to it, and use it later
But the flowers dropped in the conservatory
For this was the last day of the year
Conclusion of many ups and downs, it had begun
To be foreshadowed, leaning out into novelty
As into a bank of subtraction. The night
A dull varnish muffled the comic eagerness
Of those first steps, halted for all eternity.

Then the accounts must be reexamined,
Shifting ropes of figures. Expressions of hope
Too late, a few seconds before. Only normal
Transparent width separated them from the smaller,
Flame-colored phenomena of each settled day.
This information was like a road no one ever took
Perhaps because the end was widely known, a collection
Of ceiling fumes, inert curiosity, attacked
Rarely, and out of compunction, by millionaires
Bent on turning everyday affairs into something tragic.

Thus there was a time for all activity
As memory of regret not made known
Except as illegal pilfering on the furthest
Sketchy place of the course of a day
Which scarcely matters even for anxious
Gendarmes of these late, recent hours, now

So frequently referred to. Thus floods,
Surprising us, seem to subside
When scarcely begun. Yet so much in time for
What arrives, unnoticed our separate, parallel thought.

It is that the moment of sinking in
Is always past, yet always in question, on the surface
Of the goggles of memory. Nothing is stationary
Nor yet uncertain; a rhythm of standing still
Keeps us in continual equilibrium, like an arch
That frames swiftly receding clouds, never
Getting deeper. The shouts of children
Penetrate this motion toward, as a drop of water
Slides under a lens. Soon all is shining, mined,
Tears dissolving laughter, the isolated clouds spent.

It is appropriate that this extension is,
Has been, and always should be independent
Of elaborate misgivings concerning the future status
Of a hostile address toward each other.
Not being able to see one's way clear to
Approving ecstatic, past projects is
Equivalent to destruction of all these myths,
Wiped, like dust, from the lips. So
The weather of that day, and scalloped
Appearance of those who went by you

Are changed like mist. You see, it is
Not wrong to have nothing. But
It is important that the latter be not just
The points of disappearance, signs of the
Reduction of the little that was left, which
Disappeared all the faster because it was so little.

This part of the game keeps you for old ostracism
Long mixed with wrinkles of that horrible, blatant day
To be avoided at all costs because already known
And perhaps even more because, unlike carelessness, avoidable.

That hole, towering secret, familiar
If one is poking among the evening rubbish, yet how
Square behind you in the mirror, so much authority
And intelligence in such a miserable result.
Could it bind you because of the simplicity
Or could you in fact escape because of that limp frame,
Those conditions tumbling upward, like piles of smoke?
In that way any disorderly result is often seen
As the result of the general's fixed smile, calipers,
Moustache, and the other way was closed too.

Out of this intolerant swarm of freedom as it
Is called in your press, the future, an open
Structure, is rising even now, to be invaded by the present
As the past stands to one side, dark and theoretical
Yet most important of all, for his midnight interpretation
Is suddenly clasped to you with the force of a hand
But a clear moonlight night in which distant
Masses are traced with parental concern.
After silent, colored storms the reply quickly
Wakens, has already begun its life, its past, just whole and sunny.

Thus reasoned the ancestor, and everything
Happened as he had foretold, but in a funny kind of way.
There was no telling whether the thought had unrolled
Down to the heap of pebbles and golden sand now
Only one step ahead, and itself both a trial and
The possibility of turning aside forever. It was the front page

Of today, looming as white as
The furthest mountains, and oh, all kinds of things
Caught in that net and shaken, so often
The way people respond to things.

It had grown up without anybody's
Thinking or doing anything about it, so that now
It was the point of where you wanted it to go.
The fathers asked that it be made permanent,
A vessel cleaving the dungeon of the waves.
All the details had been worked out
And the decks were clear for sensations
Of joy and defeat, not so closely worked in
As to demolish the possibility of the game's ever
Becoming dangerous again, or of an eventual meeting.

But it was not easy to tell in what direction
The permanence tended, whether it was
Easy decline, like swallows after the rough
Business of the long day, or eternal suspension
Over emptiness, dangerous perhaps, in any case
Not the peaceful cawing of which so much had been
Made. I can tell you all
About freedom that has turned into a painting;
The other is more difficult, though prompt—in fact
A little too prompt: therein lies the difficulty.

And still not satisfied with the elder
Version, to see the painting as pitch black
Was no cause for happiness among those who surround
The young, and had expected contaminated
Fires lit by the setting sun, and sunken boats.
It seemed the only honorable way, and fertile

If darkness is ever anything else. But the way
Of that song was to be consumed, corrosive;
A surprise dragging the signs
Of no peace after it, into the disquiet of early accidents.

The head notwithstanding. A narrow strip of land
Coinciding with the riders to where
Illusion mattered no more than the rest. Flat
Walls only surrounding only abating memory.
On this new area ideas kept the same
Distance, with profiles spent into the sparse
Immediacy of excavation, land and gulls to be explored.
It was time to compare all past sets of impressions
Slowly peeling these away so that the mastered
Impression of servitude and barbarism might shrink to allegorical
    human width.

A moment of additon, then one hidden look
At it all, but it is scattered, not the outline
Of your famous openness, but kind of the sleeves
In the weather time after the doubtful present saluted.
All that ever came of it was words
To indicate any kind of barrier, with the land
Lasting beyond hope or scruple, both cell and vortex.
Further on it is a forest of mud pillars. Determined
To live, so that you and your possessions
May be dealt with at last, you forgot the other previous station.

If there was no truth in it, only pleasure
In the telling, might not others set out
Across impossible oceans with this word whose power
Was the opposite reverence to secret deities
Of shame? Or absent-mindedness? Because the first memory

Now, like patches, was worn, only as the inadequate
Memento of all that was never going to be? Its
Allusion not even blasphemous, but truly insignificant
Beside that lake opening out broader than the sun!
This, then, was indifference: it was what it always had been.

The boat stood hieratically still
On the unread page of water. No moon punching
With ideas of the majesty of crowds. A universal infamy
Became the element of living, a breath
Beyond telling, because forgetful of the
Chaos whose expectancy had engendered it, and so on, through
Popular speech down to the externals of present
Continuing—incomplete, good-natured pictures that
Flatter us even when forgotten with dwarf speculations
About the insane, invigorating whole they don't represent.

The victims were chosen through lightness in obscurity.
A firm look of the land, old dismissals
And the affair was concluded in snow and also in
The satisfaction of the outline formulated against the sky.
People were delighted getting up in the morning
With the density that for once seemed the promise
Of everything forgotten, and the well-being
Grew, at the expense of whoever lay dying
In a small room watched only by the progression
Of hours in the tight new agreement.

And they now too seem invaded, though before it was
The dancers who anticipated making unnecessary
The curtailment of one to the other. And yet,
As though this were strict premonition, their chance
Is cancelled out by earlier claims, a victim perhaps

Of its earnestness. The dance continues, but darker, and
As if in a sudden lack of air. And as one figure
Supplants another, and dies, so the postulate of each
Tires the shuffling floor with slogans, present
Complements mindful of our absorbing interest.

One swallow does not make a summer, but are
What's called an opposite: a whole of raveling discontent,
The sum of all that will ever be deciphered
On this side of that vast drop of water.
They let you sleep without pain, having all that
Not in the lesson, not in the special way of telling
But back to one side of life, not especially
Immune to it, in the secret of what goes on:
The words sung in the next room are unavoidable
But their passionate intelligence will be studied in you.

But what could I make of this? Glaze
Of many identical foreclosures wrested from
The operative hand, like a judgment but still
The atmosphere of seeing? That two people could
Collide in this dusk means that the time of
Shapelessly foraging had come undone: the space was
Magnificent and dry. On flat evenings
In the months ahead, she would remember that that
Anomaly had spoken to her, words like disjointed beaches
Brown under the advancing signs of the air.

AUTHOR'S NOTES

I wrote the group of poems called "French Poems" in French and translated them myself into English, with the idea of avoiding customary word-patterns and associations. The French version was published in the review *Tel Quel*, No. 27, Autumn 1966, Paris.

"The Double Dream of Spring" is the title of a painting by Giorgio de Chirico in the collection of The Museum of Modern Art, New York.

The title "Sortes Vergilianae" refers to the ancient practice of fortune-telling by choosing a passage from Vergil's poetry at random.